Robbery Without a Gun

Why Your Employer's Long-Term Disability Policy May be a Sham

What Claimants, Doctors, and Employers Must Know About Long-Term Disability Insurance Policies

NEW!

Seven Clauses you NEVER want to see in a disability insurance policy! (find one of these in your policy and it means your employer got hoodwinked)

Ben Glass
Attorney at Law
3915 Old Lee Highway
Suite 22-B
Fairfax, Virginia 22030
www.BenGlassLaw.com

Printed in the United States of America.

ISBN: 978-1-59571-265-3

Word Association Publishers
205 5th Avenue
Tarentum, PA 15084
www.wordassociation.com

TABLE OF CONTENTS

Does your long term disability insurance policy say any of these things?	3
Claimants without lawyers facing "loaded deck"	7
A law to protect your pension is turned on its head	8
Myths about disability insurance claims you may have heard	17
The truth about the long term disability insurance companies	19
"We are sorry your employer bought such a crappy policy"	21
Seven clauses you never want to see in a disability insurance policy	23
"We have discretion to determine benefits"	25
We will pay you if you can't perform "each and every" material duty of your occupation	30
"Own occupation" protection for less than two years	35
Income protection of less than 60 percent of prior earnings	36
We will terminate your benefits if you are able to work part-time but do not	37
The discrimination against the mentally ill	41
Limitation or refusal to pay for "self-reported" conditions	42
How to avoid falling for the insurance company traps	43
Special report for clients of Ben Glass Law	66

Does Your Long-Term Disability Insurance Policy Say Any of These Things?

- The insurance company has the "discretion" to determine your benefits
- You only get paid benefits if you can't perform "each and every" important duty of your job
- Your benefits are limited to 24 months if your disability is caused or contributed to in any fashion by mental illness, depression or anxiety
- Your benefits are not payable, or are limited, if your illness is fibromyalgia, chronic fatigue, chronic pain or any illness where the symptoms are "self reported" and thus not "verifiable" by a blood test or other diagnostic study
- Your benefits will be terminated if the insurance company says you could work part time in any job, but don't.

None of these provisions is required by any law, yet major disability insurance companies know that if they can sneak these clauses by unsuspecting employers, that they can save millions of dollars by denying or terminating valid claims.

The claims adjusters working for the insurance companies routinely use the "excuse" that:

We are sorry your employer bought such a crappy policy, but we can't pay your benefits.

Hopefully you are an employer reading this book BEFORE you make that disability insurance purchase or renew your policy. If you are a claimant who has been denied benefits, any of these clauses will increase the difficulty of getting your benefits paid. Whether you are a claimant or a health care provider who treats claimants, this book will show you the big traps the insurance company is waiting for you to fall into.

***Ben Glass*, Fairfax,Virginia**

DISCLAIMER AND WARNING

Experienced disability insurance attorneys know the arguments the insurance company will make and so should you, *before you ever stop working or file a claim*. This book reveals the insurance company arguments and sets out the mistakes claimants make. Remember, each case and every insurance policy is different and this book is in the nature of general information, not specific legal advice! Please use this book for information purposes only.

Also, please don't send me a confidential, detailed e-mail and say "what do you think?" I don't give off-the-cuff advice without thoroughly reviewing (and charging a fair fee for reviewing) your unique situation and claim documents.

If you intend to make a disability claim or have already done so, you should have an experienced disability insurance attorney on your side. In fact, this is one area of law where consumers actually do need an attorney on their side for the entire process. The entire disability insurance system is rigged against you. As you will see, respected federal judges have pointed this out time and time again.

If your claim is being made under your employer's policy, it is likely governed by ERISA (Employee Retirement Income Security Act). It is strongly recommended that your attorney have extensive experience in ERISA. Unfortunately, cleaning up the mess created by a lawyer not experienced in ERISA claims can be a very, very expensive job.

When is the best time to consult with an experience disability insurance attorney?

While you are still working and just starting to think about making a claim! You haven't made any mistakes at this point. *I have even convinced some people to stay at work because they did not have a provable disability—I SAVED THEIR JOBS (and their other benefits, such as life and health insurance) FOR THEM.* Imagine "going out on disability," losing your health insurance and life insurance benefits and then having your disability claim denied. This can lead to financial ruin.

An attorney's work becomes more difficult (and expensive) if you have made mistakes in filling out forms, giving recorded statements or if your doctor has filled out "attending physician reports" without really understanding the traps. For example, let's say your doctor has already written "no limitations" on a claim form, believing that this was necessary in order to allow you to try a few hours of work..

End result: claim likely destroyed!

Had the claimant and doctor first had the form reviewed by an experienced disability attorney, the same result (trial of working a few hours) could have been achieved without permanent risk to the claim if it turned out the employee just could not do even a few hours of work.

Claimants Without Lawyers Face a "Loaded Deck"

It's not just Ben Glass saying this. A respected federal judge has said claimants who start the disability claims process without an attorney are at a **distinct disadvantage** and often face a **loaded deck.**

> The Court also recognizes that ERISA claimants may not have the advantage of legal advice or favorable referrals before the administrative process is complete, placing such claimants at a ***distinct disadvantage*** if discovery is not permitted on judicial review. For ERISA claimants not able or aware enough to hire legal counsel before the administrative process is complete, they likely enter into judicial review facing a ***loaded deck. Abromitis v. CNA,*** (Federal Court, North Carolina.)

Finally, if you have not already done so, please read *The Truth About Lawyer Advertising* or visit www.TheTruthAboutLawyerAdvertising.com. This controversial book (controversial because some lawyers don't like what we say) has helped many consumers find the right lawyer for their case. It's available on Amazon.com.

A Law to Protect Your Pension is Turned on Its Head

The Employee Retirement Income Security Act was passed in 1974 to protect the cash in your pension fund. Today it protects insurance company profits more than it does the employees. Nowhere is this more evident than in the long-term disability insurance policy that you hold through your employer.

Ninety-nine percent of all disability insurance plans offered to employees are governed by ERISA. Under ERISA, you have the right to file suit in federal court if your claim for benefits is denied. But, unlike almost any other legal proceeding, one side goes into court with all of the "good cards." That side is the insurance company.

The Insurance Companies' "ACE"

The most important card held by the insurance companies is something called a "reservation of discretion." Don't bother looking in the ERISA statute for this "ace" – it's not there. The reservation of discretion is something that the courts have given to the insurance companies – free! Here is what this "special card" means:

If your claim for benefits is denied, you will lose your lawsuit against the insurance company, even if you are right and it is wrong, if there is *any evidence* that supports the insurance company's decision. In any other legal proceeding, you can only win if you have a preponderance (*i.e.* more than 50 percent) of the evidence in your favor. Under ERISA, however, the claimant can have 85 percent of the evidence, and the insurance company can have 15 percent of the evidence, and if the insurance policy contains a "reservation of discretion," they win!

A federal Appeals court recently put it rather bluntly:

...a beneficiary claiming procedural irregularities must show that the plan administrator, in the exercise of its power, acted **dishonestly,** acted from an **improper motive**, or **failed to use judgment** in reaching a decision.

WOW!! This court said that these cases can only be won if you can prove that the insurance company acted dishonestly!

QUICK. CALL THE POLICE. THIS IS ROBBERY WITHOUT A GUN.

Why This Book?

The first edition of this book, written in 1998, was entitled ***14 Ways to Guarantee that Your Long-Term Disability Claim Would Be Denied and You Lose in Court***. It focused on specific and preventable errors that claimants, their doctors, and their employers made in filing long-term disability claims.

In that book, I pointed out that the federal law under which most disability policies issued by employers was judged was heavily weighted in favor of the insurance company and against the insured.

Over the years, the law has not gotten any better for claimants. In my discussions with insurance brokers and employers, it became very clear that those who were engaged in the process of buying and selling disability insurance policies were not aware of the positions being taken by the insurance companies once claims were being made. In large part, they were astonished to hear the arguments that the insurance companies used to deny claims. The insurance companies were hoodwinking not only the claimants, but also everyone else along the line. The claimants, however, were the only ones to feel the pain.

It became clear that employers needed to become more aggressive at the buying stage and that insurance brokers needed to become much more knowledgeable about the group policies that they were selling.

If the law favoring the insurance companies was not going to change, what we needed were better insurance policies.

We needed employers to ask the right questions and to insist that the policies they were buying actually did provide some measure of protection to their employees. Long after courts had declared certain policies to be virtually worthless, I was still seeing insurance agents selling - and employers buying, junk policies. Apparently, the words of hundreds of court opinions were not reaching the folks who mattered most in this process.

Second, I felt that there were still obvious mistakes being made by claimants and their doctors. Many times people who did not contact an experienced disability insurance attorney until after their claim had been initially denied were shocked to get my first book, only to find that their claim was already sunk. Simple mistakes had been made early in the claim. People were selling their houses and heading to bankruptcy out of ignorance.

Thus, this new book, *Robbery Without a Gun: Why Your Employer's Long-Term Disability Insurance Policy May be a Sham*. This new book does a better job of educating the folks who are actually buying and selling the policies since without a half-decent policy, the employee has no chance for financial protection. (Please tell your own insurance agent and employer about this book. They can order it at RobberyWithoutAGun.com)

Employers, of course, have no duty to provide any disability insurance policy at all. When they do, however, a federal judge has said employers have a duty to select insurers for their employees with care, and to <u>avoid hiring insurers with reputations for shoddy and hostile claims administration</u>.

Radford Trust v. First UNUM Life Ins. Co. of Am., 321 F. Supp. 2d 226, 249 (D. Mass. 2004.) This book should help employers do just that.

Robbery Without a Gun also incorporates and revises most of the prior work which was entitled "14 Ways" and more clearly and carefully spells out what claimants and their doctors need to do to assure that valid claims for long-term disability insurance coverage will not be denied because of claimant error. It's bad enough that insurance companies have been caught cheating on claims. You don't need to help them by not getting your claim right the first time. The disability insurance companies, under increasingly intense scrutiny from courts, have gotten "smarter" about how they go about denying valid claims. Today, more than ever, claimants and their doctors must be better about avoiding careless errors in making and applying for disability benefits.

This book is now a must read for not only claimants and their physicians, but also all employers and directors of human resource entities within corporations.

Your Disability Insurance Options

Before we begin, let me leave you with this: Group disability policies bought through an employer are not the only game in town. If an employer is not going to take the time to insist that the insurance company issue a real policy with real benefits, then at least let your employees know that they can go on the market themselves and buy a policy that does provide real protection in the event of disability.

With an individual disability insurance policy, you have the right to sue and have a jury decide your claim if the insurance company refuses to pay. Your doctors will testify at trial. Your lawyer will be able to engage in 'discovery' to see how many hundreds of thousands of dollars the 'independent' medical examiners are being paid by the insurance company. Best of all, with an individual disability policy, the playing field is level, the insurance company can't hide behind the "we have discretion" shield.

With your employer's group policy, you give up all of the above.

What They Told You When They Sold You the Policy

"According to the U.S. Census Bureau, you have a one in five chance of becoming disabled. A 1997 study released by the Census Bureau reveals that more than 152 million people between the ages of 21 and 64 — the prime working ages for most Americans — have some form of disability. According to the American Council of Life Insurers (ACLI), a person age 35 is six times more likely to become disabled than die before he or she reaches age 65."

(What the HMO Case Means for Long-Term Disability Claimants)

In *Aetna Healthcare v. Davila,* the United States Supreme Court struck down a Texas law that was designed to compensate people who had been injured by healthcare decisions made by their insurance companies. Two people had sued their HMOs for failing to use ordinary care in making coverage decisions. The lower court had allowed the case to proceed.

The Supreme Court held that state consumer protection laws were completely overturned by the federal law of ERISA. Since, the Court said, the only remedy allowed under ERISA for a wrong coverage decision is to force the insurance company to pay the benefit it should have paid, a patient cannot sue the insurance company for a worsening of his condition, or for pain, suffering or death caused by the insurance company's decision.

Justice Ruth Bader Ginsburg, in a concurring opinion, said that she joined "the rising judicial chorus urging Congress and the Supreme Court to revisit what is an unjust and increasingly tangled ERISA regime." The problem, she says, is that through its decisions, the Court has made it so that virtually all state law remedies which would provide just relief are preempted, but very few federal substitutes are provided. She pointed out that a "series of the Court's decisions has yielded a host of situations in which persons adversely affected by ERISA-proscribed wrongdoing cannot gain ... relief" and that the current situation needs to be remedied "quickly" because it is "untenable."

What does this mean for long-term disability claimants? It's just more bad news. This decision reaffirms that the insurance companies who make decisions for employer-sponsored long-term disability plans are immune from suit for anything other than the benefits they already owe. Often, when disability benefits are denied, there is a cascading effect of financial disaster as pension, health and life insurance benefits are decreased or lost altogether. Moreover, workers who have been wrongfully denied long-term disability benefits often suffer enormous emotional harm in their fight to have benefits reinstated. The HMO case, however, gives insurance companies the "green light" to keep denying benefits, knowing that, on their worst day, all they have to do is pay what they owed anyway.

We join with Justice Ginsburg in urging Congress to repair this damaged scheme and to restore ERISA to its originally designed purpose of protecting, not hurting, employees.

Myths About Disability Insurance Claims You May Have Heard

(From neighbors, friends, other lawyers and insurance companies)

- **If you write the insurance company a letter and are reasonable, you will get a reasonable settlement proposal**

- **Filling out the Insurance Company form will get you your benefits**

- **If you have been awarded Social Security disability benefits, you will have no problem getting your long-term disability benefits**

- **If the insurance company sends you an "activity log," it's because it really wants to know what you do day to day**

- **The best way to convince the insurance company that you can't work at your sedentary job is for you to write a 36-page letter describing your medical condition in exquisite detail**

- **Any lawyer can help you with your ERISA long-term disability claim**

- **You should hold back your best evidence for trial**

- **Your doctors will come to trial to testify for you and convince the judge that you are disabled**

- **You will be allowed to testify at trial if your case is filed**

- **If your doctor writes that you are "disabled," then you will win your case**

- **The insurance company "appeal" process is fair and unbiased (You probably did not believe that one when you heard it.)**

- **When you file suit, the issue the judge has to decide is whether you are disabled or not**

- **You are on a level playing field with the insurance company**

- **If your employer says you are too disabled to work, the insurance company will automatically pay**

Sorry to disappoint you. None of the above is true. Read On!

The Truth About the Long-Term Disability Insurance Companies

- Insurance companies exist for one reason: to make a profit for their shareholders. Writing letters and "being reasonable" won't get you paid.

- Insurance company forms are often suited for the purpose of denying claims—asking for that information which is later used to NOT pay you, rather than asking the questions that really matter.

- Insurance companies say they don't have to pay attention to Social Security benefit awards and judges largely agree.

- An "activity log" is often used to compare what you say you did to secret videotaped surveillance.

- If you write a long 36-page "appeal," the insurance company will say "See, we knew you could work."

- There are not many lawyers who are experienced in ERISA disability claims. It's a world unto its own.

- You should not hold back your best evidence for trial, because there are no trials.

- Your doctors won't testify. You won't testify. No one will testify. There are no trials.

- Just because a doctor writes that you are "disabled" does not mean that you will be paid benefits. Insurance companies want a high degree of objective "proof" before they pay benefits.

- The insurance companies' appeal process is not fair and unbiased. Think about it. They are paying the money. They have a continued incentive to deny claims.

- You don't win your lawsuit if the judge merely finds that you are disabled. Amazingly, the judge could disagree completely with the insurance company's denial and still declare that you LOSE.

- Judge after judge has acknowledged that you are not on a level playing field with the insurance company.

- What your employer says about whether you can work carries little weight. We have seen many employers very upset to learn that the policy they bought and paid for is not paying benefits. The insurance company will say "your opinion does not count" or "you should have bought a better policy." Many employers won't let you come back to work without a doctor's release form, yet the insurance company may still say you can work. It's the ultimate financial "death spiral!" Your employer won't let you work and the insurance company won't pay benefits.

"We Are Sorry Your Employer Bought Such a Crappy Policy"

There we were, sitting in the huge conference room of the very well-heeled law firm hired by a major disability insurance company. We sat around a large, ornate conference room table.

My client, unable to work because of a number of illnesses that had befallen him, had wondered what this mediation would be like. Eighteen months earlier, his doctors had told him that he would have to give up the job that he loved because he just could not do what was expected of him anymore. They had actually been telling him to stop working for years. He had hung in there, though, because he didn't want to admit that he could no longer do the work and, frankly, he loved the work that he did. He had trusted that his employer's long-term disability insurance policy would protect him and his family in the event that the day came that he finally gave in to his doctor's demands.

Reluctantly, he had filed his claim and, despite all of the information provided by him and his doctors, his claim had been denied. He had gone through the appeals process with the insurance company, but at each step of the way, claims adjusters told him that he could work. The doctors working for the insurance company never examined him, but they did review his records and all of the reports that his own physicians had provided, and they too said, "You can work."

Left with no other choice, we had filed suit in federal court against one of the largest disability insurers in the world. Now, having gone through the litigation process, we had been invited to a mediation session. The insurance company flew in an executive from the "home office," and each side pitched in to pay half of the fee of an experienced mediator. We were all going to try to put a price on the value of my client's inability to work.

During that morning, my client got to tell his story to the insurance company executive and the lawyer the insurance company had hired. He poured out his heart to explain how he had struggled for years to keep on doing the work that he loved.

But it was the insurance company's time to talk directly to my client. Both the lawyer and the insurance company executive looked across the table. They each explained that they were "sorry" that my client had had to go through all that he had gone through. They explained that they were only doing their jobs. They looked across the table and looked directly into my client's eyes and said:

"We wish we could pay you more money, but we are sorry that your employer did not buy the best policy. We can only pay you based upon the language of this policy your employer bought. It's not our fault your employer bought such a crappy policy."

Seven Clauses you Never Want to see in a Disability Insurance Policy

While many employers do provide good, solid long-term disability insurance coverage, some policies aren't worth the cost of the fancy paper they are printed on. People are often shocked to find that even though their doctors fully support their disability and, in some cases, they have been awarded disability benefits by the Social Security Administration, their employer's plans are so bad that the insurance company does not have to pay benefits. We believe that the vast majority of these bad policies represent employers who simply have been duped by the insurance companies. Our experience is that employers and human resource personnel often have no real idea of how bad their own disability program is.

Remember, the law does not require an employer to provide long-term disability coverage, nor does it mandate the terms of any coverage that is provided. Basically, there is no federal or state oversight over policies insurance companies can offer through employers. While states can and do regulate the terms of so-called "private" policies that are offered to individuals, there is no corresponding oversight of employer-sponsored policies.

Check your disability insurance policy right now. If you see any of the following language in your policy, your policy is not protecting you the way you might think it should. Either run and scream to your Human Resources Department or run and find a private policy if you see:

- Language granting the insurance company discretion to determine benefits

- A definition of disability that requires that you not be able to perform "each and every" important function of your job before being paid benefits

- An "own occupation" period of less than two years

- Income protection of less than 60% of prior earnings

- Language terminating all benefits if you are "able to work part time, but don't"

- Blatant discrimination against the mentally ill

- Limitations on disabilities caused by so-called "self reported symptoms"

- Benefits which are contingent on securing Social Security disability benefits

- A limitation on benefits for fibromyalgia or chronic fatigue

No prudent purchaser of insurance, when they really understand what they are buying, would buy a policy containing any of these provisions. Why? Because they are buying "air." They are buying the <u>illusion</u> of protection.

Bad Language #1: The Insurance Company's Magic Shield: "We Have Discretion to Determine Benefits"

Imagine this: You make a claim for disability benefits from a major disability insurance company. The claim is denied. You are allowed an appeal of that claim, but your appeal goes back to the same insurance company that just denied your claim.

Under federal law, you are allowed to file a law suit against the disability insurance plan, but under those same laws that give you permission to file a law suit, you learn that the decision of the insurance company is presumed to be correct – you must prove that the insurance company was not just wrong, but completely wrong and unreasonable.

During the lawsuit, you are not allowed to take any depositions or ask the insurance company or its representatives any questions about how they arrived at their decision on your claim. You can't even test to see if they are qualified to determine your claim or have any experience with your diagnosis at all. You are not allowed to meet or take depositions of any of the doctors who may have been involved in deciding that you are able to work (even though they never examined you and only did a cursory review of your records). You can't find out how much money they make from the insurance company or how many claims a day they review.

When it comes time for "trial," you are not allowed to have a jury listen to your case and decide the matter based upon the evidence it hears. Instead, a federal judge will be appointed to decide your case.

The judge will not hear any evidence or take testimony from any witnesses. He will only review the insurance company's file and listen to the arguments of the lawyers.

The judge is restricted in what he can do. He does not answer the question: Was the insurance company correct in its ruling? Rather, he makes a determination about whether the process used by the insurance company to reach its decision was reasonable. He is only allowed to overturn their decision if he finds that the insurance company was wrong and unreasonable.

If he does find you are the "winner" of the case, then he cannot award you any damages for all of the inconvenience and hassle that the insurance company's decision has caused you. Lost your house? Too bad. Lost your life insurance and health benefits because of their decision? He cannot do anything about that. The only thing the judge can do if you win your case is to award you the money the insurance company should have paid you in the first place.

Unfortunately, this is not fiction. These are the "rules" that are applied when employer-sponsored long-term disability insurance plans deny your claims for benefits.

These rules are not mandated by any law or statute. They come about because insurance companies who write long-term disability policies for employers are allowed to insert into their policies the...

Six most dangerous words you will ever see in an insurance policy:

"We have discretion to determine benefits."

This is known as the "discretionary clause." What happened is, years ago, the Supreme Court of the United States decided that for disability insurance plans sponsored by employers, the insurance company would be allowed to "reserve discretion" to determine benefits. It simply decided that it would be a "good idea" to basically keep courts out of the position of being claims adjusters and to leave it to the "people who knew about these claims the best." Unfortunately, this means that the insurance companies that are going to pay the benefits have the power to add a "discretionary clause" into their own policy which, in effect, makes their decisions almost irreversible by a court.

In cases after this original decision of the Supreme Court of the United States and other federal courts, it has been decided that what this means is that the field is not level. When you go into court disputing an insurance company's finding that you are not disabled, you bear a very heavy burden to overcome that decision.

The great injustice here is that, as noted above, this clause is not required by any law. Most employers do not understand what this clause does for their employees, so they never give it a second thought when an insurance company asks that this clause be added to a policy. Most employers, sadly, never even read the policy they just bought.

All employers should immediately insist that there be no discretionary clause included in long-term disability policies, and that any such clause in a policy be removed immediately

Or else, just be honest and tell you employees you bought a crappy policy and that they'd be far better off buying an individual disability policy!

The Insurance Company Won Even After the Court Decided That it Took a Minimalist View of the Medical Records

Bradley Bingham was a paraplegic who was paid benefits for five years by Sun Life Insurance Company of Canada. After five years, his policy provided that he would only be eligible for benefits if he was totally disabled from working at any occupation.

After reviewing the evidence from Bingham's treating physicians (which supported the claim) and numerous affidavits from people who knew him (all of which supported the claim), the Court said that because of ERISA, "The question we face in this appeal is not which side we believe is right, but whether the insurance company had substantial evidentiary grounds for a reasonable decision in its favor." The Court said that the case was difficult because of "the obvious courage the claimant has shown in facing his disability."

The Court said that it was counterintuitive that a paraplegic suffering serious muscle strain and pain, severely limited in his bodily functions, would not be deemed totally disabled. The Court also said that it seemed clear that Sun Life had taken a minimalist view of the record.

Because Sun Life did not have to prove that it was right, only that it had not acted arbitrarily, the Court found in favor of Sun Life. It pointed out that even though the Social Security Administration had found Bingham to be disabled, that under this policy, establishing his inability to perform any occupation for which he could be trained, was a very high one. The Court ruled in favor of the insurance company.

In a dissent filed by one of the other appellate court judges, the judge said that there was significant and unrebutted evidence that Bingham, in his current condition, was unable to work consistently. He said that Bingham was not a malingerer, and that the affidavits submitted by his family demonstrated that if he engaged in much activity on one day, he would be in pain or discomfort on subsequent days, making it difficult for him to leave his bed. This judge also said that one would think that the Social Security finding, coupled with the affidavits from his family and the reports from his doctors that he was totally disabled, would have at least prompted the insurance company to seek an independent examination of his condition before denying benefits.

Bad Language #2: A Definition of Disability That Pays Benefits Only if You Can't Perform "Each and Every" Material Duty of Your Occupation

(In Other Words, We'll Only Pay You if You are in a Coma)

This language shows up in a lot of policies issued by Reliance Insurance Company. Other insurance companies use it as well, and for good reason. Courts have held that this language means that you will only be paid if you cannot perform "every" material duty of your regular occupation. In other words, if you were a journalist, and you were not able to travel, meet with people or type at a computer, but you could still read, then you would not be disabled from your occupation as a journalist because you could perform at least one of the substantial duties of your occupation.

In one case, the claimant was the assistant manager of computer information systems for his company. The physical requirements of his job included using a personal computer, talking on the phone, and attending meetings. He was frequently required to stand, walk and sit, and the job could not be performed by alternating between sitting and standing. He became injured and everyone agreed that his injury limited him to doing "some sedentary work for up to three hours in an eight-hour day."

Please understand what was going on here. Formerly, the claimant had worked at least 40 hours a week at a fairly physically non-taxing job. His illness, however, limited him to three hours per day, but unfortunately he was insured under a Reliance Insurance Company Policy that only paid if he could not perform each and every substantial duty of his occupation.

The insurance company argued that if he could perform even one material duty (e.g. working a little bit for three hours a day) that he was not disabled and entitled to payments.

The court bought this argument!

The court said that because of ERISA, even though "such a definition of total disability is extremely restrictive and not a disability policy that a prudent consumer would be expected to purchase, the plain language of the disability plan commands this result."

You see, under the federal law of ERISA, there is no oversight of what can be written in a disability insurance plan. Since there is no requirement that benefits be provided at all, there are no rules against providing scanty or illusory benefits.

At a hearing in this case, <u>the court likened this policy to a "coma policy</u>." In other words, it was a policy that you could only recover on if you're in a coma. The court said that while it might seem unfair that this policy paid nothing, it pointed out that the employer had paid all of the premiums and that the plaintiff had been "free to purchase on his own, a less restricted disability policy, but he did not do so." As the purchaser of the LTD policy, if the plaintiff's employer had wished to insure its employees against anything but the most serious and debilitating of disabilities, the plaintiff's employer could have elected to pay a higher premium for more inclusive coverage. Plaintiff's employer elected not to do so and the plaintiff is bound by the terms of the policy which his employer paid for.

Claim Destroyed as Court Points Out All the Errors the Claimants Doctors Made in Filling Out Insurance Company Claim Forms

In this case, *Carrigan v. Reliance Insurance Company*, The claimant's doctors called him "disabled" without knowing the policy's definition of disability; stated he could work some; and failed to show how he was different now from before when he was still working. The insurance company, on the other hand, told the judge he could he could work part time.

The court said that although claimant's Dr. Anthony described claimant as "disabled from even sedentary work," he did not set forth his definition of "disabled," and it is impossible to tell whether his definition comported with the plan's definition of total disability. Dr. Anthony also did not specify at what times or during which period claimant was disabled, and hence it is not possible to determine whether claimant suffered from the disability diagnosed by Dr. Anthony during the entire elimination period.

Dr. Darden, the orthopedist, did not give a conclusion one way or the other as to whether claimant was totally disabled. He did conclude that claimant had some physical limitations, but stated that claimant could work for approximately six hours in a work day, as long as appropriate positional changes were made.

Dr. Aiken, also, never concluded one way or the other that claimant was totally disabled. At best, he confirmed that claimant suffered from chronic back pain, and did note in

1996 that claimant's back problems could, at some point in the future, act to disable claimant from gainful employment. But he did not conclude that claimant was disabled, nor was evidence provided that the pain became noticeably worse beginning on August 28, 1998. Likewise, he provided no evidence that the back pain became noticeably worse after the date of his alleged total disability (where, before such date, he performed some of his job duties).

Claimant's vocational expert, Patrick Clifford, did submit an evaluation concluding that claimant was totally disabled under the definition of the plan. But Clifford did not specify that he was referring to claimant's condition during the elimination period, and indeed appeared, instead, to be referring to claimant's condition as of the time of his report (on or about June 23, 1999). The vocational expert did not provide any indication that he was referring to the claimant's condition during the elimination period. Indeed, to make matters worse for claimant, Clifford relied extensively on the various physicians' reports referenced above as the basis for his medical evaluation of claimant. As I noted above, these reports did not show or imply that appellee was totally disabled within the definition of the plan. By contrast, John Zurick, Reliance's vocational expert, upon reviewing some of the medical evidence, deduced that appellee could perform, at least on a part-time basis, the various duties of his job.

Bad Language #3: "Own Occupation" Less Than Two Years

Most disability insurance companies work this way: you can be paid benefits for two years if you are not able to work at your own occupation. After two years, you are entitled to benefits only if you are not able to work at *any* occupation.

The theory behind this is that two years is enough time to be able to become newly trained to be able to produce income in some business or employment.

Ninety nine point nine percent of all policies have this standard two-year protection for your own occupation. Amazingly, however, some policies afford less than two years of protection, with some providing as little as six months of benefits. What this means is that if your sickness or illness prevents you from working in your own occupation, but after six months there is some job in the marketplace that you could do, then your benefits would be cut off. Believe me when I tell you that the insurance companies work day and night to "find" a job that theoretically you would be able to do. In some cases, claimants who had no use of their arms were told by the insurance company that they could work as telemarketers with automatic dialing and voice recognition capability. It does not matter to the adjuster that the closest job may be the 11:00 p.m. to 7:00 a.m. shift 80 miles away.

Bad Language #4: Income Protection of Less Than 60 Percent of Prior Earnings

Most long-term disability insurance policies promise to pay somewhere between 60 and 66 percent of your prior earnings. This is standard. Of course, what they forget to tell you is that if your employer paid the premiums, that income taxes will still be taken out of this amount, so the protection is actually much lower. If you get social security benefits, this reduces the benefits from your employer's policy even more.

Some policies provide less than 60 percent of prior earnings coverage. Employers who buy policies with such limited coverage should be spending the money upgrading the lunch room food because after taxes these policies offer almost no benefit at all. At the very least, employees need to know that policies providing less than 60 percent of benefits are not standard and there are much better policies available on the market, probably at the same rate.

Bad Language #5: Your Benefits Will be Terminated if You are Able to Work Part Time, But Do Not

While the sales agents selling these policies focus on the benefits that will be paid if a person meets a definition of disability, hardly anyone will explain the "termination of benefits" clause in the policy. This is very, very important, as people lose their benefits because of these clauses.

The most heinous of these termination clauses says that all of your benefits will terminate if you are able to work part time, but do not. Think about this for a minute. It does not say that it will terminate benefits if you can make 60 percent of pre-disability earnings on your own. It does not say it will terminate your benefits if you can work 60 percent of the time you used to be able to work. It says it will terminate benefits if you are able to work part time, but do not.

Almost anyone could work "part time," couldn't they? Does "part time" mean an hour or two a week? We have seen cases where the medical records and the doctors all agreed that the claimant could not work more than two hours at a time during the week because of severe pain and fatigue. It is no longer surprising that some insurance companies will insist that the ability to work "up to two hours at a time" is an ability to work "part time." All they need is one doctor to say that you can do this, and the fact that you do not go out to work these hours means that all of your benefits are terminated. Remember, they do not need to actually prove that there is any employer who would hire you.

Any employer who buys a policy which allows benefits to be terminated if the claimant "can work part time, but does not" must have been sleeping when the policy was being explained to them.

The Courts Have Made it Clear that These Insurance Policies are Virtually Unregulated and the Insurance Companies can Include, or Exclude, Whatever They Want—It is Up to the Employer Who is Buying the Policy to Be Diligent

In *Smith v. Continental Insurance Company*, the Fourth Circuit Court of Appeals said that under federal law it would approve a long-term disability policy that stated "pain could never support a finding of disability."

This case sends a clear warning to America's workers that they need to review and understand their employer's long-term disability policy before they need it to see if it will truly protect them and their families in the case of a disability which prevents them from working.

Neal Smith was a vice-president of sales for J.J. Haines & Co., a wholesale floor-covering distributor. He applied for disability benefits under his company's policy after a long history of back problems and an acute back injury that occurred in January 2001.

Smith also filed for, and was awarded, Social Security benefits for his injury. Continental (CNA), however, denied that he was unable to work and refused to pay.

The J.J. Haines & Co. long-term disability policy contained several provisions that worked to greatly restrict benefits. Had Smith known how weak this policy was before he became injured, he probably would have thought twice about putting his family's financial future in the hands of his employer's disability plan if he became injured.

First, the policy gave CNA the "discretion" to determine benefits. Remember, this means that the insurance company decision is presumed to be correct and will only be reversed if it's a totally unreasonable decision.

Next, the employer was duped into buying a policy that unreasonably limited coverage to two years if the disability was one that was primarily diagnosed by fatigue, pain, headaches, stiffness, soreness, tinnitus, dizziness, numbness or loss of energy. Most group policies do not have this restriction.

Employers who truly desire to provide real financial protection need to learn how to read "beyond the glossy sales brochures" and understand the insurance policies they are buying. Otherwise, they should just stop providing the "benefit" altogether and tell folks to buy their own private polices.

Bad Language #6: The Discrimination Against the Mentally Ill

The next outrage to be aware of in long-term disability policies is the blatant discrimination against the mentally ill. Some policies limit payment of benefits if mental illness is the disability keeping the person from working. Courts have held that this blatant discrimination against the mentally ill is legal in long-term disability policies. (Remember, an employer is not required to offer any policy and courts have said time and time again that an employer can offer any policy it wants.)

Many policies go a step further, however. For example, some policies from Prudential Insurance Company limit payments for disability benefits if "mental illness plays any part" in the disability. This is a very dangerous clause. (Think about it—the one thing that almost always happens when an otherwise productive member of society gets ill and can't work is that they become depressed. Insurance companies LOVE TO SEE "DEPRESSION" in the medical records. It's their ticket out of paying you!)

Insurance companies also love to see "cognitive" problems arise out of head trauma. You hit your head in a car accident, for example. You suffer a brain injury. The insurance company will attempt to label your "brain injury" as "mental illness."

Do you see how dirty their little game is?

Bad Language #7: Limitation or Refusal to Pay for "Self-Reported" Conditions

Another outrageous limitation that appears in some policies is a limitation for so-called "self-reported conditions." Sometimes the insurance policy will list specific conditions like chronic fatigue, fibromyalgia, chronic pain, headache, migraines and the like, but other times it will not. What these insurance companies then turn around and do in denying claims is say that "there is no objective evidence that you are in pain" or there is no objective evidence that you are really fatigued. Therefore, the diagnosis is being made upon your own report of pain or fatigue and, thus, we are going to either not cover this benefit or limit it severely.

There are many well-recognized and documented diagnosable conditions related to pain and/or fatigue. There are good and expert physicians who make these diagnoses after exhaustive testing. The fact that there is sometimes not any one test or lab study that can be done to "make the diagnosis" should not be a reason for an insurance company to limit or eliminate benefits.

Note: this language is still relatively rare, but employers should be on the lookout, especially when the insurance company sends you a big batch of paperwork in advance of a policy renewal. The instinct is to not read the fine print.

Don't fall prey to this scheme. They are hoping you don't read the fine print.

So Now You Need to Make a Claim for Disability Benefits—How to Avoid Falling for the Insurance Company Traps

Mistake #1

Choosing the Wrong Date of Disability

The insurance definition of disability is contained in each policy, and each policy is different. Usually, it is a combination of an inability to work, coupled with an actual loss of wage-earning ability. This can be important in those situations where even though you may be cutting back your hours, your employer still pays you full salary. If you are still getting paid full salary, you may not be deemed disabled under your policy even if you have a substantial impairment. It is important to identify the date of disability, because all other dates (i.e., when you must file proof of claim, when payments start and when you can appeal your denial) are calculated from the date of disability.

Mistake #2
Making your claim before you know what's in your doctor's records

Insurance companies will only pay benefits if they are convinced that your medical records contain enough objective proof of disability. As soon as you file your claim, these companies will request records from your doctors (and from any doctors referenced in those records) and carefully scrutinize them.

You must get these records in your hands before you file your claim. Review them yourself! Are they accurate? Are they complete? Has the doctor recorded all of your complaints?

In one case, an insurance company denied benefits because the records of another person were included in the records sent by the doctor! Those records said all was well, and the insurance company relied on those records. (Great investigation, that was; wasn't it? The claims adjuster had so many files, she never even noticed that she was reading the wrong records.) The claimant never knew that the records her doctor sent had someone else's records in them, because she didn't get her doctor's records FIRST. It was only after she hired a lawyer and sued the insurance company that she found this out.

All of that expense and hassle was 100% avoidable by requesting the medical records before filing the claim with the insurance company.

United States Supreme Court Says Treating Doctors' Opinions Don't Count for Much In Disability Claim Disputes!

The Supreme Court of the United States ruled that long-term disability insurance companies need not give any deference to the opinions of treating physicians when evaluating disability claims.

Kenneth Nord was employed by Black & Decker as a material planner. On the advice of his physicians, he stopped working at his "sedentary" job because of hip and back pain caused by degenerative disk disease. This disease was confirmed by MRI.

Nord applied for disability benefits and was denied. He appealed the denial. His doctors and Human Resources Department filed documents supporting the claim. MetLife, the insurance company administering the claim, sent Nord to a neurologist for an examination. While agreeing with the diagnosis made by the treating doctors, the neurologist said that Nord was capable of sedentary work if he took his pain medication and had "some walking interruption in between" work.

Despite the support of his physicians and Human Resources Department, his appeal to MetLife was denied! He sued.

When his case was reviewed by the Court of Appeals, that court ruled that the insurance company had to justify its rejection of Nord's treating physicians' opinions. Since there was no justification for rejecting the treating physician's opinion, the Court of Appeals declared Nord the winner.

The United States Supreme Court reversed and held that the disability plan did not have to give special weight to the opinion of the treating physician. The court reasoned that nothing in ERISA or the Department of Labor's regulations governing long-term disability claims mandated that the insurance company give any special deference to a treating physician.

The court reached this ruling, despite recognizing that:

It may be true that the treating physician, as a rule, has a greater opportunity to know and observe a patient as an individual; and

Physicians repeatedly retained by benefit plans may have an incentive to make a finding of not disabled in order to save the employer's money and to preserve their own consulting arrangements.

Astonishingly, the Supreme Court admitted that, "The validity of a claim to benefits under an ERISA plan is likely to turn on an interpretation of the terms of the plan at issue" (and, I say, not necessarily on whether a person is actually disabled)."

Obviously, buying one of the crummy policies will get you crummy coverage.

Mistake #3
Stopping Work on the "Wrong" Day

To an insurance company, the last day worked, or ***LDW***, is a very important date. Much of its investigation of your claim will revolve around the medical, vocational and financial facts in existence as of that day. Unfortunately, many people stop working on the well-meaning - ***but legally incorrect*** - advice of doctors, supervisors, co-workers, family or friends. As much documentary evidence as possible must already be in existence on your ***LDW,*** because an insurance company will ask the following questions:

How come the person stopped work on ***LDW*** when they worked eight hours the day before and 40 hours the week before that?

What does the medical evidence show? Was there any objective medical evidence proving a change in condition between the LDW and [pick any arbitrary recent time period.] Even if you have some dreadfully debilitating disease and have worked *through it* for years, the insurance company is likely to say, ***well, yes, you have a dreadfully debilitating disease and most people would have stopped long ago—*** ***BUT YOU DIDN'T—SO WHY ARE YOU STOPPING NOW?***

The answers to these questions can and should be found in the medical records BEFORE you file.

You may have very good answers to all of these questions, but why risk trying to ***fill in the blanks*** later, ***after your claim has been denied***, when you can take care of these issues now?

One man quit work and applied for benefits, even though his doctor's records did not say he was disabled. He lost his job, his health insurance and was properly denied disability benefits.

Mistake #4

Assuming that Your Employer Says You are too Sick to Work, Will be Enough for Your Insurance Company

Remember that either you or your employer has purchased an insurance policy. Therefore, in almost all cases, the money that may be paid to you for your ***long-term disability*** comes from the insurance company. It is that company, ***not your employer***, which determines when you meet the legal definition of disability under the terms of the insurance policy. We have seen cases where the employer would not let the employee come back to work ***without approval from the doctor*** and yet the insurance company would not pay the benefits! ***How can this be?*** The answer is that most insurance policies insure an ***occupation,*** not a ***job.*** This means that while you may not be physically able to do all of the specific job requirements of your employer, you might still be able to perform the ***substantial and material duties*** of your occupation.

Mistake #5

Not Understanding Your Policy Before You File Your Claim

Insurance polices can be hard to understand. You should obtain and review your policy before you file your claim. If your policy is an employer-sponsored policy, you should obtain both the ***Summary Plan Description (SPD)*** and the ***insurance policy itself*** before you file your claim. Both of these documents should be available from your employer. The **Employee Retirement Income Security Act (ERISA)** requires that these documents be made available to you upon written request to the ***plan administrator.*** If you have a private policy and cannot locate it, call your agent. You can obtain a replacement policy (usually for a small fee) from your insurance company. Whether you have an employer-sponsored plan or a private policy, ***make sure you obtain and read all amendments and endorsements to the policy.***

Warning: Little Known Insurance Policy Provision Ends Orthopedist's Long-Term Disability Payments Early

A decision from the United States Court of Appeals for the Fourth Circuit sends a clear warning to any physician who is currently receiving disability benefits under a long-term disability insurance policy. This decision affects physicians in Virginia, Maryland, West Virginia, and North Carolina.Virginia Beach orthopedist Paul Krop was insured under a group long-term disability policy issued by AIG Life Insurance Company. After Krop sustained a partial disability in January 2000, he filed a claim for benefits. His claim was filed under the "partial disability" provision of the policy because, while he was no longer able to operate on a full schedule, he was able to maintain an office practice. Thus, he had suffered a significant reduction in income.

AIG ultimately agreed with Dr. Krop and began to pay benefits. Each month, Dr. Krop received income from his group orthopedic practice. The policy had been bought by the practice in part to make sure that any physician whose income was diminished would have that diminution "made up" by the insurance policy. The policy provided that if in any month the partially disabled physician's income was between 20% and 80% of his pre-disability average monthly income, benefits would be paid.

Dr. Krop's monthly income was based in part upon the income for the entire group. When his income in a month exceeded 80% of his pre-disability income (because the group as a whole had a good month), Dr. Krop thought that his disability payments would be suspended for that month.

The insurance company, however, took the position that Dr. Krop's disability benefits permanently ceased, even though he had the same disability and even though he may not be able to earn anywhere near 80% of his pre-disability income at any time in the future. Dr. Krop's position before the court was that he still had years of benefits available to him for those months in which his own income was less than 80% of his average pre-disability income.

In an opinion that shocked attorneys who represent claimants in long-term disability claims, the Fourth Circuit Court of Appeals upheld the lower court's decision that, indeed, the "good month" that the practice had caused a permanent end to Dr. Krop's long-term disability payments.

This case sends a clear message to anyone receiving long-term disability insurance benefits to make sure that they fully understand the policy. If a claimant is working and receiving partial disability benefits, then other income must be aggressively managed to prevent a permanent and unnecessary cessation of benefits.

Mistake #6
Trusting the Advice of the "Human Resources" Department

Oftentimes employees have been taught to take all questions about benefits, including long-term disability benefits, to the ***human resources*** department. This well-meaning advice can be fatal to your claim if the advice you get is wrong. We don't suggest that your own employer would deliberately mislead you, but our experience tells us that (1) most human resources personnel are not legally trained in the interpretation of insurance policies and (2) human resources generally has no pull whatsoever with the insurance company. Again—unless the employer is actually funding the monthly benefits (and this is a ***rare*** occasion), it is the insurance company that is protecting its own assets. Our experience, based upon reviewing many insurance claim files, is that no amount of pleading by your employer will influence an insurance company that wants to deny benefits to you. ***You*** need to take ***personal responsibility*** for your own claim!

Mistake #7
Using Only Insurance Company Forms to Document Your Claim

When you make a claim for benefits, the insurance company will send claim forms for you and your physician to complete. Typically, the physician forms will have questions such as: ***How much can this person lift; How long can they sit; Can they walk long distances?*** These questions are irrelevant to many claims. The doctor will dutifully answer the questions the insurance company asks, but later the insurance company will say that those answers ***just weren't enough information!***

You should sit down with your doctor (after having reviewed your own records fully), explain the terms of your policy, and get your doctor to set out fully in a report why your sickness or illness prevents you from performing the ***substantial and material duties of your occupation***. The doctor may charge you for this report. ***Pay the charges!*** It is far better to have a well-documented claim ***from the beginning*** than to have to go back, ***after you have been denied benefits***, and justify your claim. Also, if you have been denied benefits and are appealing your claim, you and your doctor will have a limited time (as defined in your policy) ***within which to submit additional reports***. Why be under ***time pressure*** when all of this work can be done ***before you ever submit your claim?***

We Are Not Kidding About This Terrible Law! It's Not who has the Better Case if you Sue; It's "Can the Insurance Company State It's Case Without Laughing?" If so, it Wins.

Ivan Kimber suffered from insulin-dependent diabetes. After he lost vision in one eye, he was transferred from his job as a heavy equipment operator to a desk job. Over the next three years, his condition worsened. After suffering several incidents of diabetic shock, his doctors recommended that he take medical leave and apply for disability under his company's long-term disability plan.

At first, the plan granted him benefits "indefinitely." Later, the plan changed its mind and terminated those benefits. Kimber submitted reports from three doctors. The plan again started to pay, but stopped after Kimber reached 24 months of benefits, citing the 24-month Mental and Nervous provision in the policy.

The Court said that under the law, the insurance company did not have to be correct to win. The insurance company's reasoning for denying the claim only had to be "slightly reasonable." The court also said that if the policy was ambiguous, the insurance company could interpret it any way it wanted. (Under "real" insurance law, ambiguous insurance policies are interpreted, by law, against the insurance company.)

The Court looked at all of the facts in the case and said that "although we might have come to a different conclusion, the plan administrator acted within his discretion in [denying the claim]."

Mistake #8

Leaving Work Without Calculating Your True Monthly Benefit

Most long-term disability policies only pay 60 to 66.6% of your monthly salary. This would make some sense if the insurance company's check to you was tax-free, but it usually isn't. Taxability of disability benefits should be a major concern to you. Generally speaking, if your employer paid the premium on the policy, then the insurance payments to you are taxable. If you paid the premiums, then they are tax-free. Also, you need to understand what the payments will be based on. What if your income fluctuates? Is a substantial part of your income based on commission, bonuses or profit sharing? Each policy is different and since this can have a major financial impact on your family, you need to understand the payment structure before you file your claim.

Mistake #9
Doing Things Your Doctor Says You Shouldn't Do

It goes without saying that you shouldn't try to cheat the insurance company. Our law firm has "fired" clients who we felt were trying to cheat the insurance company. No good lawyer represents cheaters!

Understand that they will find you out. That van down the street just might have a video camera hidden inside. We've got a stack of videos from insurance companies in our office.

! Alert 1

If the insurance company sends you an "activity log" for you to fill out, it is a sure bet they have put you under surveillance. They are NOT looking for your report on what you can't do. They are looking to inconsistencies between that report and what their spies tell them.

! Alert 2

If the insurance company sets up a so-called "independent medical examination" for you or even seems particularly interested in when your next doctor's appointment is, be very aware. Best practices would be to go straight to and from that appointment. No shopping, no nothing. Also, be very aware that as you leave the doctor's office for one of those "independent" exams, they may be watching you out the window! Yes, if you walked slowly into their office, you darn well better be walking slowly when you get back out to the parking lot.

You are being watched.

Mistake #10
Using the Insurance Company's Lawyers to File for Social Security

If the disability insurance company pays you long-term benefits, you will usually be required to file for social security benefits. If you win your social security case, you will usually be required to ***reimburse the insurance company and further benefits will be reduced*** by the amount of the social security payment.

If your dependents receive social security benefits ***because of your disability***, you payments will also be reduced. (Great deal for the insurance company, isn't it?)

Many insurance companies will offer you the services of their lawyers (or an affiliated law firm) to file for and pursue your social security benefits. Don't use them. In too many instances, these lawyers have steered the social security claim towards a disability that is favorable toward the insurance company, a mental condition which limits the insurance company's payments to two years, for example. We have also seen situations where an insurance company lawyer who is representing a claimant in social security ***quits the case while he is supposed to be representing you before the Social Security Administration*** because while he is working to get you benefits, the disability insurance company terminates your benefits anyway.

We sometimes get the impression that they are only working to recover the benefits for the insurance company. We don't have any proof of that, but why risk the apparent conflict of interest? You should hire your own experienced social security lawyer. (That won't be me—but I can refer you to someone who is!)

Finally, even though the insurance company may provide the social security attorney to you ***free***, it's not the great deal they make it out to be. In most cases, if you get your own social security attorney and pay their fee, this amount will be deducted out of the money you are required to pay back to the insurance company. So, you really don't pay any more to get your own independent attorney.

Mistake #11
Hiring a Lawyer Not Experienced In Disability Insurance Litigation

A new client told me recently, "You guys are hard to find." I asked him what he meant and he told me that he had searched for a long time before he found an attorney who specializes in disability income insurance litigation. Unfortunately, there are just not many of us out there.

Litigation of a long-term disability insurance claim is different from litigation of an automobile accident claim. It is different from many other contract claims. The world of insurance dispute litigation has its own body of case law, history, procedure and terminology. Your attorney should know, before the case begins, what you will need to prove in order to win your case. You should look for an attorney experienced in disability litigation.

If you have an employer-provided disability insurance company, you need an ERISA-experienced disability insurance attorney. Nothing less will do.

Mistake #12

If Your Policy Came Through Your Employer, Not Making Sure Your Attorney is Experienced in ERISA

ERISA is the Employee Retirement Income Security Act of 1974. This federal law was originally designed to protect your retirement pension, but today it governs just about every aspect of any employee welfare benefit, including life, health and disability insurance. ERISA has a special rule for just about every step of the disability insurance process. It sets out the timeframes within which insurance companies may initially decide claims, give you documents that you request and decide your appeals. Most importantly, the law of ERISA controls what evidence you will be able to present to a judge if you file suit, and what standard of review that judge will use. In short, your attorney must understand both the law of disability insurance and the law of ERISA.

We recently reviewed a case where the claimant, a doctor, paid over $12,000 to an attorney to "research" his claim. This attorney started at ground zero, learning, frankly, information that he could have gotten right out of this book.

See, the attorney thought the doctor's claim was huge, with punitive damages and all that. He researched the heck out of the case.

It took me ten minutes to read the insurance policy and tell the doctor that he had one of those crappy policies that only protected him for two years. He ended up selling his "retirement home" and going back to work!

Mistake #13
Handling Your Case Without Legal Help

Of all of the different types of legal cases out there, this is one where you really shouldn't go it alone. Buying this book was a great decision on your part, but if you are going forward with your claim, at least consult with an experience disability insurance attorney.

I know, I know, you are saying that Ben Glass is an attorney and, of course, he would say that you need a lawyer. Well, I sincerely hope that you do not need an attorney, but I also hope that you will at least consult with an experienced attorney ***(Anyone! It doesn't have to be me)*** before dealing with the insurance company yourself. But if you need more proof that it just may be helpful to have an attorney, remember that the whole process is, by nature, adversarial. ***Your claim takes assets from the insurance company.***

If you have to go to court, the judge is going to look at the record that the insurance company developed while it was denying your claim. Even the best disability attorney in the country can't always make a winner out of a crummy record.

The insurance company has no incentive to develop a record favorable to you. Think about it.

Mistake #14
Missing Your Deadlines

In a long-term disability claim, there are deadlines for (1) filing your *notice of claim*; (2) filing your *proof of claim*; (3) filing your *administrative appeal* if your claim is denied; and (4) filing your lawsuit if your administrative appeal is denied. The time limits are found in your policy and in your jurisdiction's law.

Since the deadlines are determined by the cansuar of the policy, not the law, each case is different. It is important that you check your own policy for the deadlines.

Special Report for Clients of BenGlassLaw

Even though the insurance company may have denied your claim, many cases do settle once suit is filed against the insurance company. We've prepared a special report on the settlement process. We'd rather not reprint it here because we know that some of the major insurance companies have bought this book.

If you become a client, we'll make sure you get a copy of our Special Report on Settling Your Long-Term Disability Claim.

Get Additional Copies of the Book

Your friends, your insurance agents and your employer should have a copy of the book.

Visit RobberyWithoutAGun.com for ordering information.